12 THINGS TO KNOW ABOUT
WILD WEATHER

by Jamie Kallio

www.12StoryLibrary.com

12-Story Library is an imprint of Peterson Publishing Company and Press Room Editions.

Produced for 12-Story Library by Red Line Editorial

Photo Credits: Mike Siedlik/AP Images, cover, 1; Lane V. Erickson/Shutterstock Images, 4; Shutterstock Images, 5, 12, 14, 16, 21; Patryk Kosmider/Shutterstock Images, 6; Alexander Kuguchin/Thinkstock, 7; Mike Hollingshead/AP Images, 8, 28; Thinkstock, 9, 10, 18; David J. Phillip/AP Images, 11; Yasushi Kanno/AP Images, 13; Deyan Georgiev/Shutterstock Images, 15; Giulio Napolitano/Shutterstock Images, 17; Corbis, 19; John Carnemolla/Thinkstock, 20; Igumnova Irina/Shutterstock Images, 22; Vadym Zaitsev/Shutterstock Images, 23; Dan Brandenburg/Thinkstock, 24, 29; Rashid Valitov/Shutterstock Images, 25; Chris Cafferkey/Thinkstock, 26; Jan Mika/Shutterstock Images, 27

ISBN
978-1-63235-035-0 (hardcover)
978-1-63235-095-4 (paperback)
978-1-62143-076-6 (hosted ebook)

Library of Congress Control Number: 2014946813

Printed in the United States of America
Mankato, MN
October, 2014

Go beyond the book. Get free, up-to-date content on this topic at 12StoryLibrary.com.

TABLE OF CONTENTS

WEATHER CAN BECOME EXTREME

Will it rain? Will it be warm? What should I wear? Weather is often the first thing people think about every day. Weather is the state of the atmosphere at a particular time and place. In most places, the weather can change from season to season and day to day. It may even change from hour to hour.

The National Weather Service (NWS) in the United States helps people prepare for the weather. The NWS uses radar on the ground. It has satellites in space to gather weather information. It also uses weather balloons to measure air temperature, pressure, wind, and humidity. Together, all this information gives them weather forecast reports. Forecasts may predict sun and warm temperatures. Or, they might predict extreme weather.

The weather forecast lets drivers know about dangerous weather.

What is your weather today? Is it normal or extreme? Use these pages' definition of extreme weather to help you decide. Give two examples of how your weather is normal or extreme.

The NWS also issues weather watches and warnings to alert people of dangerous weather. A *watch* means conditions outdoors may possibly turn dangerous. People should keep a watchful eye on the sky. A weather *warning* means dangerous weather is occurring now. People should seek shelter and take other safety steps.

Weather warnings are very helpful in the case of extreme weather. Extreme weather is weather that is more violent or different from normal. Heat waves, high winds, and extremely cold winters are all examples of extreme weather. Some

1,000

Average number of weather watches the NWS issues each year.

- Weather is the state of the atmosphere on a given day.
- Weather can change from season to season, day to day, and hour to hour.
- The National Weather Service provides forecasts.
- Weather watches and warnings help people stay safe during extreme weather.

hurricanes may also be considered extreme. While extreme weather may not happen very often, it causes damage to buildings and roads and puts people at risk.

°C °F

50 — 120

40 — 100

30 — 80

20 — 60

10 — 40

0

— 20

10

— 0

20

— 20

Heat waves can be harmful to human health.

5

2

A THUNDERSTORM IS AN ELECTRICAL STORM

Approximately 18 million thunderstorms occur each year. At least 2,000 thunderstorms are in progress at any given time on Earth's surface. Thunderstorms bring much-needed rain to many places. They also produce electricity.

A thunderstorm is a rainstorm that produces lightning, thunder, wind, and sometimes hail. Some severe thunderstorms can cause tornadoes. A thunderstorm forms when warm, moist air rises from the earth. As the air rises, it cools down. Cool air holds less water than warm air.

Thunderstorms bring rain to farm fields.

THE WORLD'S LARGEST HAILSTONE

Hailstones are a form of frozen precipitation. They fall in hard, irregularly shaped balls. They usually range from the size of a penny to the size of a softball. Larger hailstones can cause damage to crops, windows, and cars. The largest can kill animals and humans. The largest hailstone on record fell in Vivian, South Dakota, in 2010. It was almost the size of a bowling ball!

Lightning strikes in rural areas and in cities.

Some cool air turns into clouds. Eventually, the cool air in the clouds falls as precipitation.

Thunderstorms also produce lightning. Lightning is a giant electrical spark in the sky. It heats the air five times hotter than the surface temperature of the sun. Most lightning viewed by people is a spark between the sky and the ground. Lightning can also travel between clouds. During a thunderstorm, lightning often targets the tallest object in an area.

10

Number of minutes a typical thunderstorm takes to develop.

- About 2,000 thunderstorms are in progress at any given time on Earth.
- Thunderstorms can cause lightning, thunder, wind, hail, and even tornadoes.
- Lightning is a giant electrical spark in the sky and is extremely powerful.

Lightning is extremely powerful. Lightning that strikes the ground can deliver enough electricity to light a 100-watt light bulb for up to three months. It can cause severe electrocution in humans and animals. Approximately 100 people die every year in the United States from lightning strikes. During a thunderstorm with lightning, people should find shelter. They should stop outdoor activities, such as soccer and swimming, until the storm passes.

TORNADO WINDS CAN REACH 300 MILES PER HOUR

Tornadoes touch down more often in the United States than in any other country. They begin as thunderstorms. Some thunderstorms turn into violent, rotating columns of air that extend from the storm to the ground. If a tornado does not touch the ground, it is called a funnel cloud.

Tornadoes put vehicles—and the people in them—in danger.

Tornadoes form most often during the spring and early summer. They build up quickly, usually blow through a small area, and die out within a few minutes to an hour.

Most tornadoes are weak. But even small tornadoes can have wind speeds between 65 and 110 miles per hour (105 and 177 kph). But especially severe ones can reach wind speeds of 300 miles per hour (483 kph). Tornadoes can cause serious damage. A powerful tornado can lift cars, animals, and people into the air. It can destroy almost everything in its path. The speed and force of its winds can knock over buildings and trees. Objects can be thrown far through the air.

If the weather forecast includes the possibility of tornadoes, it is time to be alert. The sky may turn a dark greenish color before a tornado develops. If there is a funnel cloud

8

1,200

Number of tornadoes that touch down in the United States each year.

- Tornadoes touch down more in the United States than in any other country.
- Most tornadoes form quickly, blow through small areas, and die out within a few minutes.
- The safest place to be during a tornado is in a basement or other underground area.

THINK ABOUT IT

Are tornadoes common where you live? Use the Internet to research how often tornadoes occur in your state. Then, use these two pages to help you create a tornado action plan for your family.

Go below ground when a tornado warning is issued.

and a loud roaring noise, seek shelter immediately. The safest place to be during a tornado is in a basement or other underground area. A small, windowless room, such as a bathroom, is best if a home has no basement.

RAINING FROGS

On June 28, 1957, in Thomasville, Alabama, a rainstorm came through. With the rain also fell thousands of frogs, fish, and crayfish. Most likely, the animals had been sent into the sky by a powerful tornado that hit 15 miles (24 km) away.

4

HURRICANES ARE POWERFUL TROPICAL STORMS

Like tornadoes, hurricanes are powerful storms. However, most hurricanes cause more damage and injuries than tornadoes do. They are larger, last longer, and cause other extreme events, such as storm surge. Most hurricanes strike in August and September. However, a hurricane can develop anytime between June and November.

Hurricanes are strong tropical storms. They are a type of cyclone, or large, rotating thunderstorm. A hurricane's winds can reach 200 miles per hour (322 kph). Most hurricanes are 200 to 300 miles (322 to 483 km) across. Many get larger and stronger as they travel.

Hurricanes form over warm ocean waters and have a warm core. They mostly occur in warm areas of the

This satellite image shows the rotation of a hurricane.

North Atlantic Ocean and the eastern North Pacific Ocean. Most last for just a few days, but some can last for two weeks. Most hurricanes die out once they reach cooler ocean waters. Traveling over land also weakens a hurricane. Land cannot supply the heat and moisture to keep the hurricane strong.

When hurricanes hit land, they bring lots of wind and rain with them. Their winds can destroy houses and rip trees from the ground. One of the most dangerous effects of a hurricane is a quick rise in sea level. This is called storm surge. During storm surges, winds drive ocean waters to shore. Storm surges cause many coastal areas to flood.

In the United States, peninsulas and other coastal areas are at risk of being hit by hurricanes. Some of the deadliest hurricanes have struck the shores of the Gulf of Mexico and the Atlantic coast. Towns and cities there are home to many people. When Hurricane Katrina struck the Gulf Coast in 2005, more than 1,800 people were killed.

In 2005 Hurricane Katrina severely flooded parts of New Orleans, Louisiana.

100

Average number of people killed in the United States during hurricane season.

- Most hurricanes are 200 to 300 miles across.
- Hurricanes usually die out over land, but can bring heavy rain and winds.
- Storm surge is one of the most dangerous effects of hurricanes.

TSUNAMIS ARE AS FAST AS JET AIRPLANES

The word *tsunami* comes from the Japanese word for "harbor wave." A tsunami is a seismic sea wave. It can cause massive destruction when it reaches a harbor or shoreline.

A sign warns people to seek high ground if an earthquake triggers a tsunami.

Sometimes earthquakes under the ocean cause tsunamis. When these earthquakes happen, the sudden movement of the ocean floor causes the water above it to move. The movement starts the rolling waves that will become a tsunami. The waves of a tsunami can be over 100 feet (31 m) tall.

Other times an underwater landside or volcanic eruption can produce a tsunami. Both cause large pieces of land to fall into the ocean. The land displaces the ocean water around it. The ocean adjusts itself to make room. This adjustment creates the tsunami.

Tsunami waves start very small. They may only be a foot (30 cm) high. But that changes as they get closer to shore and enter shallower water. They slow down and start to grow in height and power. Tsunamis can travel across the ocean at 500 miles

12

per hour (805 kph). That is nearly as fast as a jet airplane. At this speed, they can cross the entire Pacific Ocean in less than a day.

As a tsunami gets closer to shore, the crests of its waves grow higher and higher. The waves flow onto shore as violent floods. Their impact can destroy buildings, trees, and most other structures in the way. Many tsunamis develop without warning. This causes much loss of life.

Flooding and fires in Natori City, Japan, after a tsunami caused by the Tohoku earthquake

164

Height, in feet, of a tsunami that hit Sumatra, Indonesia, in 2004.

- A tsunami is a seismic sea wave that can cause severe damage when it reaches shore.
- Tsunamis are typically caused by underwater earthquakes.
- Tsunamis can race over the ocean at 500 miles per hour (805 kph).

TOHOKU EARTHQUAKE

On March 11, 2011, the Tohoku earthquake struck off the east coast of Japan. The earthquake was the fourth largest in the world and the largest in Japan. Tokyo's residents received one minute of warning before the earthquake struck. Tsunamis followed, with waves reaching 128 feet (39 m) high and stretching 6 miles (10 km) onto shore. More than 18,000 people were killed, mostly from drowning.

HEAT WAVES CAN BAKE FRUIT ON TREES

More people die from heat waves each year than from hurricanes, tornadoes, and floods combined. A heat wave is an extended period of high temperatures and humidity. They can last days or even weeks. Weather scientists use criteria to determine if a heat wave has occurred. They consider two or more days of temperatures 10 degrees higher than normal a heat wave.

Cities are especially at risk for heat waves. Urban asphalt and concrete surfaces store heat longer than plant-covered surfaces do. At night this heat is released, causing increased nighttime temperatures. This is called the urban heat island effect. To escape the heat, people run their air conditioners. But the energy needed to run the air conditioners results in more heat. This makes the problem worse.

Extreme heat can cause serious health problems in humans. Heat exhaustion causes increased heart rates and heavy sweating. A more serious condition, heatstroke, occurs after the symptoms of heat

People in cities use fire hydrants to stay cool in a heat wave.

Crops, such as these grapevines, suffer during heat waves.

exhaustion go untreated. Heatstroke occurs when the body's temperature gets too high. It is life threatening. People and animals are not the only things to suffer in a heat wave.

7,500

Number of people in the US Midwest who died during a heat wave in August 1988.

- Heat waves usually occur in the summer and can last for weeks.
- More people die from heat waves each year than from hurricanes, tornadoes, and floods combined.
- Heat waves are occurring more frequently.

Vegetables and fruits do, too. High temperatures put stress on fruit trees. The leaves of the trees and the fruit can get sunburned. In extreme cases, the fruit will bake on the trees. During a US heat wave in 2012, corn and soy crops suffered costly damage.

Heat waves have become more frequent and longer lasting around the world since the beginning of the twentieth century. The Intergovernmental Panel on Climate Change points to global warming as the cause. As the earth's temperature continues to rise, heat waves will become more common. Extremely hot summers are predicted for every part of the United States, with the worst heat occurring in large cities.

15

DROUGHTS ARE SLOW KILLERS

A drought is a long period of time when no rain falls. They can happen in all regions of the world. But they are more common in dry areas. Droughts are slow to begin, last a long time, and end gradually. They can last a few weeks or a few years.

Droughts do not occur suddenly. They depend on weather conditions. Drought can occur when there is a disturbance in the hydrological cycle. The hydrological cycle controls how water is stored in and released by clouds. Air patterns in the atmosphere move the water in unexpected directions. This can cause drought in areas expecting the precipitation. Poor farming practices, overgrazing, overpopulation, and climate change also can cause drought. The global temperature of Earth has been steadily rising over the last 150 years. Scientists predict this rise will cause more droughts in the future.

Drought can kill off crops, including corn.

Farmers in the sub-Saharan country of Niger struggle with drought.

Water shortage is a main concern when drought occurs. Little or no rain causes plants and other vegetation to dry up. Soil becomes drier. Surface water sources dry up, too. Lack of water can harm humans and animals and damage crops. This can lead to famine. Drought and famine have been severe throughout Africa. Since the late 1960s, the region south of the Sahara Desert has experienced a prolonged drought. It has led to approximately 100,000 deaths. Thousands of starving people migrated from the region. In the United States, droughts cost $6 billion to $8 billion every year.

11 million
Number of people worldwide killed by droughts since 1900.

- Drought can happen in all regions of the world.
- Changes in the hydrological cycle, poor farming techniques, and climate change can cause droughts.
- Drought and famine have been particularly harsh throughout Africa.

17

DUST STORMS CAN MOVE ACROSS OCEANS

Dust storms look like giant, dark, cloudy walls moving through the landscape. A dust storm is a strong whirlwind. Strong winds carry the dust over long distances. Dust storms in the Sahara Desert in Africa can be carried across the Atlantic Ocean. The dust from these storms reaches the Caribbean and the eastern United States.

Dust storms are not exclusive to the desert, however. They can happen in any dry, hot area where loose dirt or sand can be picked up easily by strong winds. All this dust and debris

A dust storm sweeps across Phoenix, Arizona.

can be very dangerous. It reduces how far people can see. This makes driving dangerous. The dust can cause poor air quality and can trigger breathing and other health problems. The storms can interfere with telephone and cable TV lines. They even block sunlight. If someone gets caught in a dust storm, he or she should stay in the car or find shelter until the storm passes.

A dust storm gathers over a street in Kansas in 1937.

25

Wind speed, in miles per hour, of an average dust storm.

- Dust storms require dry conditions and loose dirt, dust, or sand particles that can be stirred up by strong winds.
- Dust storms move fast and occur without warning, and they can cover long distances.
- Dust storms are dangerous and can affect vision, air quality, and telephone and cable TV lines.

THE DUST BOWL

During the 1930s, the US Great Plains suffered a long period of drought and dust storms. The whole region became known as the Dust Bowl. A massive dust storm hit the area on April 14, 1935. This storm was known as the Black Blizzard. Ninety-seven million acres (39 million ha) were affected by the Dust Bowl.

WILDFIRES BURN LARGE AREAS QUICKLY

Wildfires are extremely destructive. They burn buildings and crops, harm people, and cost billions of dollars to fight. But wildfires are also an important part of nature. Some wildfires can be helpful to the environment. They remove dead or decaying matter and kill off diseased plants and harmful insects. They burn thick canopies of leaves so more sunlight can get through to new plants. When they come in contact with civilization, however, wildfires can be dangerous and costly.

Wildfires, also called forest fires, are destructive blazes that start in forests or brush areas. Many wildfires are caused by lightning strikes. Others are caused by

Wildfires can threaten homes and human life.

humans. Wildfires can happen anywhere. They are common in the forests of Canada and the United States. In the United States, western states usually experience the worst wildfires. In southern California, wildfires are often more intense due to hot, dry Santa Ana winds. Regardless of where they start, wildfires can last for weeks. They can burn across thousands of acres of land.

Three elements must be present for a wildfire to start: fuel, oxygen, and a heat source. Firefighters refer to these conditions as the fire triangle. Dry weather and drought turn green plants into flammable fuel. The heat source can be lightning, embers from a campfire, or even a dropped cigarette. Strong, dry winds feed oxygen to the wildfire as it spreads quickly over land. Firefighters fight wildfires by removing one or more of the elements in the fire triangle. They spray water and fire retardants on flames and clear nearby vegetation so the wildfire runs out of fuel.

Firefighters hold back wildfire flames.

100,000
Number of wildfires each year in the United States.

- Wildfires need the fire triangle—fuel, oxygen, and a heat source—to form.
- Wildfires are caused by lightning strikes or human actions.
- Some wildfires can benefit the environment by burning up dead plant matter, which lets sunlight reach new plants.

BLIZZARDS WHITE OUT THE LANDSCAPE

In a whiteout, snow blows so hard that it is difficult to tell the sky from the ground. Whiteouts occur in severe winter storms called blizzards. During a blizzard, temperatures drop and snow falls. Winds over 35 miles per hour (56 kph) blow the snow. This reduces how far a person can see. It also creates drifts that can block roadways. People driving through a blizzard are in danger of losing their way. They can also become stranded on roads. If they get lost in the cold, they could get frostbite. In many cases, people have died from the cold.

A blizzard occurs when a mass of cold air moves out of the Arctic or Antarctic and meets warmer, moist air. With blizzards come very cold temperatures. In the United States, the National Weather Service (NWS)

Driving during a whiteout can be very dangerous.

defines a severe blizzard as winds blowing more than 45 miles per hour. In the United States, blizzards usually occur between December and March.

Blizzards can be extremely dangerous. Traffic slows down as roads become slick and covered in snow. Drivers cannot see in the whiteout conditions. Car accidents are common. For similar reasons, airports and railroads usually close down. In homes pipes freeze and electricity goes out. Blowing snow can drift over cars and even buildings.

50

Depth, in feet (15 m), of snow drifts along the US East Coast after a blizzard in March 1888.

- In a whiteout, blowing snow makes it difficult to tell the sky from the ground.
- People stranded outdoors during a blizzard run the risk of frostbite or even death.
- Blizzards close down roads, airports, and railroads.

Snow drifts are a common sight after a blizzard.

ICE STORMS TAKE OUT POWER LINES

An ice storm is a heavy downpour of freezing rain. Freezing rain occurs when temperatures are below freezing, or 32° Fahrenheit (0° C). The rain freezes when it hits the ground. This covers roads, sidewalks, and other surfaces in ice. This ice coating is called glaze. Most of the glaze is only an inch (2.5 cm) thick, but even this small amount is dangerous.

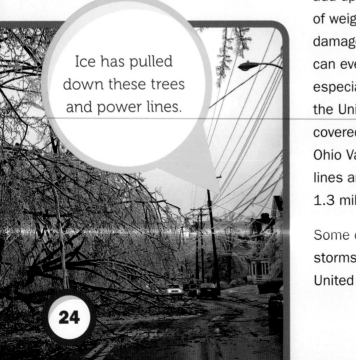

Ice has pulled down these trees and power lines.

Glaze-covered streets and sidewalks make travel difficult. The glaze makes these surfaces very slick and slippery. Vehicles can lose control and spin out. People walking may slip and fall. Glazed tree branches and power lines are especially dangerous. They can be up to thirty times heavier than normal when covered with glaze. Just half an inch (1.3 cm) of ice on a power line can add up to 500 pounds (227 kg) of weight. Extra weight increases damage to trees and power lines. It can even cause them to collapse, especially when winds are high. In the United States, a 2009 ice storm covered northern Arkansas to the Ohio Valley. It glazed over power lines and knocked out power to 1.3 million people.

Some of the most damaging ice storms occur in the southern United States. This region usually

Ice storms can cover vehicles in an icy glaze.

80

Percentage of Maine residents who lost power in a January 1998 ice storm.

- Ice storms are heavy downpours of freezing rain.
- The ice that coats trees, cars, streets, and power lines is called glaze.
- Ice storms that hit the southern United States cause the most damage.

experiences a warmer climate. Warm-weather buildings, crops, and people are not prepared for severe winter conditions. The worst ice storm in the United States struck the south in 1951 from January 28 to February 4. The combined damage in Mississippi, Louisiana, and Arkansas cost millions of dollars. Twenty-five people died.

12

COLD WAVES CAN FREEZE WATER SUPPLIES

The National Weather Service defines a cold wave as a rapid drop in temperatures within 24 hours. It lasts at least two days with temperatures 15 degrees below normal. However, cold waves can last for weeks. A cold wave develops when cold air masses move over a large area. The

> Cold waves can be difficult for outdoor animals.

longer a cold air mass stays in place, the colder the temperature becomes. Often high winds accompany cold waves. This lowers the temperature even more.

Cold waves pose risks to humans and animals. A person may experience frostbite or even hypothermia. Cold waves can cause long travel delays. When bodies of fresh water freeze, travel by boat is disrupted. Ice can form on the wings of airplanes and must be removed before the planes can fly. During cold waves, people stay warm by using electric heaters and other heat sources that can cause fires. Cold waves interfere with firefighting. The cold can freeze the water in

THINK ABOUT IT

Use two or more sources to learn about other animals that go into hibernation during times of great cold.

26

fire hoses, and ice on streets and sidewalks makes it difficult for firefighters to reach fires.

Livestock that live and feed outdoors can be hurt by the cold. Their water source can freeze over. Fruits and vegetables can suffer

People in the midwestern United States experienced extreme cold in the winter of 2013–2014.

53

Number of days the Minnesota cities of Minneapolis and St. Paul experienced temperatures at or below 0° F (-18° C) in the winter of 2013–2014.

- A cold wave is when temperatures are 15 degrees below normal for two days in a row.
- If outdoors for too long during a cold wave, a person can experience frostbite and hypothermia.
- Cold waves can cause significant damage to agriculture and livestock.

during cold waves in regions that are not prepared for such weather. In January 2007, California farmers lost $1.4 billion during a cold wave.

THE POLAR VORTEX

The winter of 2013–2014 was one of the coldest on record in the central United States. That is because of a change in a weather pressure system called the polar vortex. Usually the polar vortex stays over the Arctic. But in the winter of 2013–2014, it weakened. This allowed cold air to move south into the United States. Climate scientists are researching to learn if global warming caused the change.

27

FACT SHEET

- Most people seem very interested in the daily weather. To help people prepare for their day, the National Weather Service (NWS) in the United States provides weather forecast reports. In cases of extreme weather, the NWS also issues weather watches and warnings to alert people of danger.

- At least 2,000 thunderstorms are in progress at any given time on Earth's surface. About 18 million thunderstorms occur each year. Some thunderstorms create tornadoes. Tornadoes touch down more in the United States than in any other country.

- Wildfires are wild, traveling blazes that can happen anywhere but are more common in the forests of Canada and the United States. A fire needs fuel, oxygen, and a heat source. Most wildfires are caused by humans.

- Whiteouts occur during blizzards when blowing drifts of snow turn the landscape completely white. During an intense blizzard, all modes of transportation tend to shut down completely until conditions are safer. An ice storm covers everything in its path in an icy coating of glaze. Glaze is extremely heavy; just half an inch of ice on power lines can add 500 pounds of extra weight.

- Cold waves can last for days or even weeks. When skin is exposed in extremely low temperatures, frostbite can happen quickly. The most important precaution a person should take when going outdoors during a cold wave is to wear a hat and scarf. Thirty to fifty percent of one's body heat is lost through the head and neck.

GLOSSARY

climate change
A long-term change in a region's typical weather patterns.

crests
The highest points of a wave.

famine
A lack of food for large numbers of people.

forecast
A prediction scientists make about what weather will happen in the future.

frostbite
A physical condition in which parts of the body freeze.

hail
Pieces of ice that fall from clouds like rain.

humidity
The amount of moisture in the air.

hydrological cycle
The sequence water takes as it enters the atmosphere as water vapor and falls to the ground as rain, ice, or snow.

hypothermia
A physical condition in which the temperature of the body drops dangerously low.

precipitation
Water that falls to the ground as rain, snow, sleet, or hail.

seismic
Movement relating to or caused by an earthquake.

severe
Intense, extreme, or dangerous, when describing weather.

30

FOR MORE INFORMATION

Books

Close, Edward. *Extreme Weather.* New York: PowerKids, 2014. Print.

Mogil, H. Michael and Barbara G. Levine. *Extreme Weather.* New York: Simon & Schuster Books for Young Readers, 2011. Print.

Simpson, Kathleen. *Extreme Weather: Science Tackles Global Warming and Climate Change.* Washington, D.C.: National Geographic, 2008. Print.

Websites

The Old Farmer's Almanac for Kids
www.almanac4kids.com/weather/index.php

Tree House Weather Kids
www.urbanext.illinois.edu/treehouse/index.cfm

Weather Wiz Kids
www.weatherwizkids.com

INDEX

About the Author

Jamie Kallio is a youth services librarian in the south suburbs of Chicago. She received an MFA in writing for children and young adults from Hamline University in Minnesota and is the author of several nonfiction books for children.

READ MORE FROM 12-STORY LIBRARY

Every 12-Story Library book is available in many formats, including Amazon Kindle and Apple iBooks. For more information, visit your device's store or 12StoryLibrary.com.